COLD SOUL

AN ANTHOLOGY OF MODERN POETRY

COLD SOUL

AN ANTHOLOGY OF MODERN POETRY

Dr U.S. Saranya

First Published, 2018

Published by

Kalpaz Publications
C-30, Satyawati Nagar,
Delhi – 110052
E-mail: kalpaz@hotmail.com
Ph.: 9212142040

Printed at: G. Print Process, Delhi

Cataloging in Publication Data—DK
Courtesy: D.K. Agencies (P) Ltd. <docinfo@dkagencies.com>

Cold soul : an anthology of modern poetry / [editor], Dr U.S. Saranya.
pages cm
Poems.
ISBN 9789386397706

1. Indic poetry (English)—21st century. I. Saranya, U. S., editor.

LCC PR9495.25.C65 2018 | DDC 821.008 23

Contents

Foreword

Poetry is a language and it is most distilled and most powerful as Poetry is considered to be the crown to literature. A poet is before anything else a person who is passionately in love with the language. It gives me immense delight to introduce this book written by young poets to the world. The outburst of thoughts and feelings poured in the form of poems express the innate talent within them to the outside world to relish and cherish. This modern poetry collection talks about the best teacher, efforts of a father, women safety, hopes and dreams, love, humanity, religion and so on. If I were to generalize about the poets in this remarkable anthology, I would want to say something about the tone of this book. There is noticeably a common voice or approach. This is not just a collection of rhyming words, lyrics or dissociated rambles. The poems are set in a noticeable voice aware that it is speaking, pondering, puzzling, that are unspoken or shocking. As stated, it is a funny world ready to blame but the pen in the hands of these poets has showcased the best in them. My hearty wishes to Dr.U.S.Saranya for her love for literature and for compilation of this work and I wish the journey of the budding poets to continue in multiple volumes.

Best wishes.

Dr. P. Malathy
Assistant Professor,
Department of English,
Chikkaiah Naicker College,
Erode-4

Preface

Poetry is a creative form of literature and some people feel that a poem should be in a prescribed way for people to read. For years together we have seen people writing poetry with proper meter, rhythm, alliteration adding to it and so on the list goes by. This anthology in your hands breaks the proper form of writing poetry and makes it simple and easy for the readers to read and understand the artistic work of the young minds. This book consists of 61 poems which voices out the various forms of creative, imaginative and real life incidents into words for the readers to enter into the world of literature. This trend was started much before where in the poetry tried to sound like prose and writing in free verse became much popular among the readers and many poets wrote this way.

This anthology is an attempt to popularize the modern poetry yet in a natural and traditional way as it combines the best elements of traditional and modern poetry. Majority of the poems in this anthology is metered and rhymed as per the new formalism form of poetry and some are free versed too as to make it go with the flow. This anthology will definitely be more accessible and easy for the readers to read and enjoy the modern form of poetry of the creative minds.

Acknowledgement

Most importantly, I express my earnest sense of gratitude to my parents G. Sadhasivam and S Umarani whose vision made me realise the true value of education.

I would like to thank my VIT family for inculcating and motivating me to have a vision to achieve big and giving me the freedom to learn and grow as an individual. My sincere thanks to Dr G Vishwanathan, Chancellor VIT University, the Vice Presidents, Assistant Vice President Kadambari S Viswanathan, Vice Chancellor Dr. P. Gunasekaran, and Registrars Dr. Dr. K. Sathiyanarayanan VIT Vellore and Dr. R. Padmanaban VIT Bhopal and my heartfelt gratitude to Dr, B, Sathis Kumar for his support and guidance.

I would like to express my deepest gratitude to my contributors for bringing out this work without them this work would not be possible. I would like to thank my brother Mr. U.S.Prassanna Raj and my dear sister in law Dr. P. Lakshmi for providing necessary feedback and encouraging comments which helped me bring this book out effectively. I express my sincere thanks to my friend K.Karthik for constantly supporting me with positive words and bring out this book on time.

About The Contributers

Dr. U.S. Saranya: working as Assistant Professor of English, School of Advanced Sciences and Languages, VIT Bhopal University.

Abhijith Mohan: "I was born to an army man, and have been traveling with him across India since childhood. My love for literature and poetry started at the age of 14. I love putting my heart on pages, and I believe in living free."

Neha Trivedi: "Being born to a father, an officer in BSF, I was afforded with a plethora of opportunities of voyaging across many locales extending to the remotest corners of India. Mind ingrained with scenic beauty and rich cultural heritage of diverse societies prompted me to pen my experiences at the tender age of 13. Keeping the passion alive, I wish to go further, higher and beyond in times to come by creating timeless marvels."

Ayush Jaiswal: "I belong to KanpurI love writing down my observations and my life experiences. I like writing because I feel that when speech fails, words speak significantly."

K. Karthik: Former Head of the Department of English in Maharaja Co-education Arts and Science College, Erode. Presently he is working as an Assistant Professor in Bharathidasan College of Arts and Science, Erode.

Birthday Wish to My Beloved Hero

Dr. U.S. Saranya

Sincere and simple man you have been
Such a man i have never seen
Teaching you say is your profession
The way you do it make me feel that it is your passion
Entering into forty three in 2017
Let your success grow like a banyan tree
Wishing you on this auspicious day
For thousand more years to stay
I do pray to god to give you happiness
And keep your health with utmost fitness
Before you, success is not far miles
Forever i want to see you succeed, with smile.

Incredible India

Dr. U.S. Saranya

Where my country is going on?
Things happening can't be borne;
One side, people ruthlessly being killed,
Everywhere the lifeless dead bodies being filled.

One side, innocents being attacked with gun,
We, people, keep watching with fun;
Visiting going on between counterparts,
Discussing, that are all mere apart.

Ours, not be a place to live,
People soon will keep on leave,
Infants, for food, carrying luggage,
Pathetic; their conditions are in young age.

It is not a place for our sisters,
Oh God! They are in horrible sinister;
Those days, they were all fired,
Bearing children all year and got tired.

A woman be a Divine spirit and a flower,
That's why they are done deflower?
Guilty, here, is never punished,
So doing, they get cherished.

Nature is only in picture,
Our eyes have nothing to capture;
Keep on doing deforestation,
That's why I get frustration.

That's why we call it "Incredible Nation" That is without even a single notion.

You-Loneliness

Dr. U.S. Saranya

Never in my life felt sadness,
Until I had your joyful guideness;
Lost in life, my almost happiness,
And have fallen into loneliness.

Thousands upon thousands were around me, Felt nothing, but single loneliness;
Tutor taking classes before me, Listened nothing, but unheard loneliness.

Neighbours playing funs with me,
Smiled never, but serious loneliness;
Companions talking with me,
Heard nothing, but mute loneliness.

Having forth me sumptuous food,
Tasted nothing, but bitter loneliness;
Feel like sleeping in every night,
Slept never, but sleeping loneliness.

Having many ways and miles to walk,
Walking nowhere, but standing loneliness;
Feel like having bright future,
Carry nothing, but doom loneliness.

Almighty, get you back my loneliness, And give you back my happiness.

Miles to go before My Sleep

Dr. U.S. Saranya

Miles to go before I sleep,
Never even a single time, I get wept,
Because miles to go before I sleep.

Have forth millions to get achieved,
So have no time to have rest,
Despite never want to get worried.

Want to live a sophisticated and cosy
Life; have main things to get,
So every time in the quest, I am busy.

Hurry to sleep in a comfortable coach,
Do spend unlike others, sometimes others too;
In no mood and moment and others to watch.

Want my precious land to be fertile,
Praying to have smiles forever,
Urge to go for meeting and party with cocktail.

Longing to get a superb sum,
Desired to have a hand full of wages
Anyone is there to get only some?

Miles to go fore I sleep -to my beloved,
Have forth millions- to have happiness
Do have main things- to get loved.

Have to sleep in a cosy couch- in mum's lap,
Want large land to be being - papa to be young ever.
Praying to have a long smile - in my siblings' faces.

Have a must for a meeting- with my friends,
Longing to get superb sum -a superb sum of hug
These are the miles that have no ends.

Desire to a heavy earning- from my children,
Only these things, I want more;
To possess this, let me start to run.

What a Funny World

Dr. U.S. Saranya

When you remain silence
Everyone shows to you violence;
To them, doesn't be patience
Show an agile performance.

They tell, "Talk less, and work more"
I tell you, "Talk more, and work most";
And get your own right
With that make everything right.

All are ready to blame
To them, show your fame;
Always be an inflammable,
And show that you too can able.

Solve the problem one by one,
Prove the problem to everyone,
I utter you, "Don't take rest"
Because, forever you are the best

What I Gain Is....

Dr. U.S. Saranya

I ran as if to meet the moon,
But I realised where I am soon;
Came to know, money is nothing,
To give and get love is everything.

Without anything, I am waiting here,
Only for money I am going there;
Paradise is lost; Hell is regained,
To come here, I bargained

Years ago, this was my passion,
Here often I lose my patience;
For gaining this wealth,
I have lost my health.

My fellows make me laughed,
You make my sorrows lost;
Don't know how to tackle,
All are here notoriously fickle.

This is not a place to flourish,
All are showing their rubbish;
Making little things exaggerated,
This is not to be greeted.
Advising me to change myself,
But try to mind yourself.

Coffee

Neha Trivedi

I love how your aura blends into mine, ameliorating the burdensome and stressful days.

It feels euphoric when my fingers run through your body, exploring your fine curves.

How your cherishing warmth gives me a miraculous sense of comfort and security, fading away all my anxiousness.

I adore how beautifully you wear your bold dark shades.

It is ecstatic when the elixir contained within you kisses into my lips, sliding under my neck, illuminating my soul with a purpose that had been lost under the ruins of shattered hopes and believes, leaving me flooded with motivation.

Dearest steaming mug of coffee,

I love you.

One Day

Abhijith Mohan

One day,
You'll wake up again.
Not because the nightmares called.
But I called.
You'll see me by your side.
My tousled hair,
My morning eyes,
My gaze, and my palm on your cheek.
I'll make you get lost,
In our maze of dreams.
I'll kiss you back to life,
As I fall in love with you, again and again.

Dada Ji

Neha Trivedi

That evening he sat on a wooden stool in the verandah,

Admiring the kids playing on the streets,

Wearing his worn out vest and dusky trousers.

I watched him holding his old and overused steel coffee mug with his wrinkled, bony and exhausted hands, shivering because of his depleting physical health.

He slightly pursed his crinkled tan lips and blew into the hot coffee before slowly sipping it in.

He was drowned into a satisfying suffocation of loneliness,

Embracing in close to his heart, all his desires to be heard, understood and recognized as being important by his very own family;

The family that blossomed because of the hardships he faced throughout his life.

His eyes were looking for some company, maybe a person to chat with, to listen to his tales about the good old days.

I kept my phone aside and sat beside him, smiled and watched him light up when I said,

"Aaj koi story nai sunaenge aap Dada jee?"

Voyage of my Fading Existence

Aayush Jaiswal

Sometimes I go back and visit the locked house of our memories And I replay each scene back to back

The remnants of your fading existence in my life burns my chest

And I wonder if I could have done any better than I did

Maybe you and I deserved to be this way

Maybe we were meant to end in pain and desperation,

To watch ourselves crumble helplessly, and end being alone But still I see you smiling each day,

I see you laughing and more alive than you ever were It's not like I do not want you happy, I do but I wonder why I could not be like you

Why can't I just forget all that happened and move on with my life?

Why can't I be smiling and joyous again?

But then again, I am me and I can't change that

Neither can I change the things that passed away

I guess this all is just supposed to be this way.

The Empty Corridor

Abhijith Mohan

One fine day, I walked into an empty corridor.
The corridor smelled of my favorite coffee.
It smelled of books, old and new.
It smelled of the rain, alleviating the souls.
Then I realized why.
She was standing there,
Waiting for me.
Waiting for heaven.
Little did she know,
I was searching for the same.
That's how our paths crossed, we were candles.
Lights of hope in each other's darkness.

Denizen of the Past

Neha Trivedi

The night breaks in and her half asleep consciousness drifts off to the bitter and sweet memories,

Dancing to the rhythm of the moonlit sky and twinkling stars,

Leaving behind smiles sprinkled with innocence and moistening the warm pillow that rests under her head.

The days they spent together are buried in the depths of time but she undesirably continues to be a denizen of the past.

A Cold Soul

Aayush Jaiswal

Scared, she screamed for help
It was a bleak building
She heard nothing but herself
Men running after her, trying to tear her clothes
Mistaken they were, she is not a whore
Another minute she was caught, thrown to ground
And she begged god to defend her from these hounds
But in those dark corner no demi god came
That night she became victims of the untamed
The world motivate her to be thankful of being still alive
Inhumanly she was asked humanly she sobbed
Little did they know
Alive was her body but soul
Her soul already died....

The Talisman

Abhijith Mohan

The warrior was dauntless,
His life was his battle, and death an easy escape.
Every day he fought, without his shield,
Sword in his hand, challenging death.
Blood and sweat smeared across his dark face.
His beard hid his battle scars.
But his eyes had the truth.
He fought with no fear,
As he had a shield,
Not of the man's metal.
But the universe immortal.
For she prayed to the universe.
And he always came back.
With a smile unknown to the realms of men.
Her love was his shield,
And he's safe,
Forever.

Insomnia

Neha Trivedi

I lay in my bed with my eyes closed, listening to the tenor bells of my passionately thumping heart.

With flashbacks that are reminiscent of the successes I had lost and the failures I had won,

I envelope my chest in the arms of my knees and hug my pillow tight in a hope to appease the agonizing hollowness of my soul.

I feel my senses going numb, exhausted for being denied the passivity they deserve,

Denying to hold on, slipping into nothingness.

Letting go of the insomnolence, I finally fall asleep.

Is this Called Love?

Aayush Jaiswal

Is this called Love?

When the two sit together.

When the two talk all blether.

Is this called Love?

When the two hold each other's hand.

When the two are promiscuous to take each other's stand.

Is this called Love?

When the two look each other's eyes.

When the two are plighted to die.

So,

Does the love doesn't mean

To have respect

Clear thoughts.

And not to have disrespect and blear thoughts.

Does the love doesn't mean

To be contented of what u have.

And not to be contended for what u got.

Does the love doesn't mean

To love for the sake of love.

And not to prove fake in love.

The Lady

Abhijith Mohan

My college sweetheart, is no doll.
She's a tigress,
Feisty and bold.
She has those eyes,
The double edged sword,
One edge love and another glare.
Terrified I'm, of that stare.
For her Love is magic,
And I can't stay away.
She is no girl to be guarded.
Lord have mercy if you take her for granted.
A sweetheart she is, but only for me.
Stranger you are warned,
Play with fire, and you get burned.

Her

Neha Trivedi

Every day she wakes up with her iridescence brighter than the sun, wearing her best attire furbished with a new confidence, drenched in the fragrance of her quixotic hopes, she walks out illuminating the brutal world.

In no time her spring turns to autumn,

and her spirit gives in to the bitterness of the cold. Each time she feels them touch her with their eyes, she withers,

still dauntlessly fighting the stares of famished men all young and old. Somewhere the majestic tigress succumbs to their glares, and she's carved into an anxious soul.

Recede

Aayush Jaiswal

Nights passed by toss and turns,
When exhausted memories retreats,
Wrought my heart full of burns,
Fashioned by a pinch of salt treats,
Consigning to drink water of Lethe,
I promised to recoup by love faiths retract,
But fallen again into seethe,
This is my absurd heart's fact,
Perhaps it is time to dance with dalliance,
It is time to dance out and recede,
It is time to dance with ambience,
Perhaps it is time to dance out and decease.

One Night

Abhijith Mohan

A craving we have,
For one night's sleep.
A night in the present,
A night without tears,
A night without death.
A night with peace,
A night with sleep,
For those who fell,
Have seen it all.
The infernos,
Burning the skin to bone.
The maze never ends,
The wounds never heal,
For the night returns, every day.

Introversion

Neha Trivedi

I tread on the unattractive and depleted path of introversion,

Leading towards the door of wisdom that opens into the land of enchantment and bliss.

Wrapped into rags, barely covering the barrenness of my soul,

I abandon the greed for material desires.

I am numb to the worldly attention,

For I choose to observe than to be observed.

The corners are my home,

Providing me with windows to admire the diverse shades of personalities worn by men, trying to conceal their true identities.

I tread on the path of introversion, seeking for the unanswered and unknown, carrying with me, only my hopes,

Because I, being poor, have nothing but my dreams.

Wade through or Couch In

Aayush Jaiswal

Soggy noon it was,
All faces were pale!
But the beauty of nature,
Surpasses all grave!
There was no breeze,
Still loving spell dwells!
With no mouth to say,
Speaks thousand words of jewels!
A perfect place to choose,
To uncloud all mourns, all your delusion flews..
When floret ingest all groans!
So,
Learn to fight every day,
As small shivery stem does.
Learn to Enjoy every day,
As small Fluttering Leaf does!
Learn to shine every day,
As small wayward dew does!
Learn to bloom everyday as small fragile flower does!

My Hopes

Abhijith Mohan

Someday,
She will be mine.
Someday,
I'll be fine.
Someday,
I'll be complete.
Someday,
I would breath.
Someday,
She'll know,
Of what I have in me,
And what it means.
Someday,
She'll be mine.

Lie With Me

Neha Trivedi

Lie with me under the wide blue sky,

With daffodils around us ambling with the morning breeze.

Hold my hand and close your eyes,

For the beauty is felt more than just seen.

Tell me your secrets and unfold your lies,

Your highs, lows and all the places you've been.

Unmask your soul, strip off your disguise,

Your wit, your virtues and all your sins.

All the flaws that you cherish and the zeniths you despise.

All your fascinations and dreams foreseen.

We the Puzzles

Abhijith Mohan

We all are puzzles,
Incomplete ones.
Living our own adventures,
To find the missing pieces.
Some we find in light,
Some find us in darkness.
One way or the other,
The pieces come together.
To help one soul,
Breathe fully.
We are never alone,
There's always someone out there,
Waiting for us,
The same way we are waiting for them.
In time, we meet.
And we live.

Eyes

Neha Trivedi

Look into my eyes and you'll see the stars,
The flesh and spirit stained in scars.
Ambitions, falls and the dreams bizarre,
And the struggle how I made it this far.
You'll see my armor,
You'll see my soul prepared for the war,
The rage that keeps me from falling apart.
Look into my eyes and you'll see the stars,
The flesh and spirit stained in scars.

Lust

Neha Trivedi

There she goes flippin' her long ebony hair, I'm a lover and she's the rain.

There she goes flaunting her charisma arcane.

Men her curves making them go insane,

And I'm thirsty for the elixir from her love fountain..

I'm bewitched for her beauty is an enslaving bottle of champagne,

Damn she goes flippin' her long ogling and ebony hair,

I'm a lover and she's the rain.

May be I am Falling in Love

Neha Trivedi

Maybe I am getting lost in the empty corridors,

With your arms wrapped around my waist,

Wearing the wreath of your warm, tranquil pecks.

Maybe I am loosing myself into the undiscovered fathomage of passion when your lips kiss into mine.

Maybe I am letting go of the dark, eagerly waiting to be blinded by the light of your dazzling, baffling eyes.

Maybe I am ready to follow your lead,

Dauntlessly deepening my trust in you.

Maybe, I am in love.

The Human

Abhijth Mohan

The dark that comes and envelopes me,
No more I'm a prey to it.
I wear my failures with pride now.
I myself become the dark.
I no more cower in the shadows,
For I now sit on the throne itself.
I'm the King now,
And I'm the death,
I'm the dark,
And I'm the life.
I'm me,
I'm the human.

Meditation-Detachment from the Material World

Neha Trivedi

That night I lay on the grass,

Gazing at the night sky,

Drifting into the silent brilliance of this universe,

Reaching for the horizon entwining the materials with spirituality.

My weightless soul slowly floating through the energies,

Exploring the undiscovered higher dimensions.

Finally, I surrender myself to the divine calmness,

Breathing in the radiance that illuminates my burdened spirit, Guiding me to the abode away from the darkness of ignorance.

The Last Rite

Abhijith Mohan

When my time comes,
I would have seen them live.
As I sleep, as I let go,
I'll take the depths and dive.
My fight will end, so will my quest,
My eyes will stop, so will my clock.
And I'll see you as I rest,
Smiling beneath that rock.

My Precious

Neha Trivedi

Looking outside the window, watching the time passing by, I felt the vertigo driving my consciousness to the past.

The sleepless nights spent dreaming of the equinoxes I longed for in my somberly stagnant life,

For my heart being wretched, hoped for equal shares of darkness and light. Startled by the warm merry chuckles of my precious, recocheting back to reality,

I realized that I finally found my abode where the light isn't eternal but darkness doesn't haunt me anymore.

Her Eyes

Abhijith Mohan

I saw those eyes, again in the lake.
The boat, my memories.
The water my past.
The eyes that once lit my flames.
She was magic, like the morning dew.
Her words music, but they were few.
Her smile was heaven, my salvation.
Her hair was silk, an incarnation.
She left as she came,
Like an evening breeze.
But as love was born,
I let the time freeze.

My Religion

Neha Trivedi

My religion does not define my spirituality.

I preach the supreme and worship karma.

My soul knows no name that personifies my God.

He is never confined to a statue or a book or a charm,

he dwells in the core of an atom and in the energies wandering across the multiverse.

He is not the creator of my fate and neither will he destroy me.

He is the iridescence in the dark,

the limitless horizon of opportunities and possibilities.

He is the unexplored, stained in the blots of religion.

He is the faith that drifts beyond the brilliance of mankind.

He is the undiscovered Almighty.

Dauntless

Abhijith Mohan

The story of me, is of no glory.
It's no tale, of triumph and glamour.
My words for you, ends with sorry.
For I am no knight and I have no armor.
I am an adventure, a dreamy one.
For the mounts under me, ain't done.
I have seen the clouds kissing the hill.
I have been to valleys, with deathly chills.
It's the path I chose, long ago.
When I was a kid, who never said no.
I live to taste the wines of old, to further dive in fables untold.
You may not see the beauty in here,
For it takes a heart, not just eyes.
Do not come close, don't be near,
For you oh sir, wants to be in ties.

Share a Coke with Me

Neha Trivedi

When you think of the texts that make you fiddle, And the short smiles exchanged,

When exchanging glances isn't enough and you want to call out my name, When you see me hunch in the college lobby,

When you're suspicious of being secretly captured by my phone,

When you want to relive my awkwardness, for such moments come and go. When you regret saying no goodbyes before you had to flee,

Don't fret sweetheart because I'll be at the cafeteria, And you can share a Coke with me.

The Cries of the Lonely House

Neha Trivedi

I woke up to the aroma of old cardboard boxes,

heaped up in the store room, eagerly waiting to be wrapped on to our aged, drab hued, walnut wood furniture.

Tiny dust particles bathing into the flare of daylight that pierced through the window cracks, illuminating our shadowy room.

I walked bare feet into another room and witnessed the windows mourning for their separation with the elegantly dangling curtains.

I heard the lamenting walls, narrating the ballad of the traditional Rajasthani paintings which used to lay on its chest.

I saw how the wise old glass shelves which once displayed my father's mementos and souvenirs, swallowed their misery into a dull silence. Transfers were indeed difficult, for us and for our soon to be lonely house.

Summer Love

Neha Trivedi

Thank you sweetheart for your summer lucent love, for the times she hid her tears in the rain.

Thank you for the desolate autumn when her heart withered, and for the dark, malevolent winter days in pain.

Now her severed spirit is mended with gold and with spring you shall see her blossom again.

She Let him go

Neha Trivedi

She felt her hands turning cold,

And her breath went slow.

The scenes reminiscent of her bitter-sweet life flashed before her eyes,

And the blood rushing within her veins calmly seized to flow.

Death being her last embrace,

this time she let him go,

For with her doom she shall put an end to all his sufferings and sorrow.

Soul Mate

Neha Trivedi

It's hard to find a soul that fathoms mine,
Who unravels the darkness that I've devoured with time.
That one rebel who disregards the world's paradigm,
Extricating me,
letting my mind and heart entwine.

My Winter Walk

Neha Trivedi

I walked through the dew drenched forest of darkness which was chaotically freckled by sunlight beams exuding through the canopy of the dense, redolent sandalwood trees.

I walked into the dusk enveloped in thick layers of fog, into the silent night concealed by a calm, cold and dark shroud beautifully imitating death.

I walked through the skin numbing breeze, desperately seeking warmth, For my spirit has been turned brittle by the merciless frost.

I walk in the winter with a hope to find my aurora, shielding my blemished yet zealous heart.

How Many Times

Abhijith Mohan

How many times you have seen those promises wither with time.

How many times have you hated yourself for letting your faith get stolen.

How many times you tried to drown yourself in tears, yet held on to your life.

How many times you died inside every time you pushed goodness away.

How many times you felt that after death was heaven and life the real hell.

How many times you wished for all that to be not true.

A wish for everything to be not euphoric but smiling.

How many times you fought yourself just to love another.

How many times you tried to punish him for crimes of some other.

Let it out sweetheart,

let him into your heart.

He's different, he's harmless.

How many times you have wanted to love him the way he loves you.

How many times you wanted his chest to be near you.

How many nights you wanted him to be the sentinel.

Gather up your courage,

And love again.

For this time, he's no monster.

He's a child in a man, who loves you with heart.

He's a dreamy eyed light,

Who wants to be the one.

Stag and the Doe

Abhijith Mohan

The wounded Doe,
Kept running still.
She never healed,
For she ran from the kill.
She had to be like the wind.
Stopping not, and moving on.
Then she stopped, for a stranger stag.
The stag then made, her stay intrigued.
And healed her, without consent.
He stayed there, guarding the Doe.
For he found the precious,
He has to live for.

Traitor

K. Karthik

We dined, lived, and travelled with,
I believed you, adored you, had faith
In you and become together at the end.

Once we decided to travel together,
And I, the idiot, waited for you thither;
At last, came you not, only your call,
Said you, somewhere else you fall.

Thought you only for your future,
Didn't know that you would torture;
Because of you, I fallen in hell,
With never knowing how to get well.

You are mother, father, counsellor,
Teacher, at last nothing but only traitor.

Lover

K. Karthik

When we were playing in road,
Came an auto with some heavy load;
The playing boys, to see you, turn'd towards,
Stunn'd at once and to explain, have no words;

You, the beauty of beauty, got down,
Seeing your splendid beauty, we fell down,
Witness'd you, the pretty Goddess, our face,
That so our life got precious grace;

Never observ'd you, the White Cleopatra, all,
You, Cherubim, wore, attire with red shawl;
Did look at me and did smile,
I, your slave, was arrest'd for while;

Came you, the Siren, beside to mine,
Call'd my life, to make me fine.

Mother

K. Karthik

No man born of his own,
In womb some seeds have sown;
For almost fourteen score days,
You had been in sad and gays;

Nor in womb I did vomit but
You; had nights without eyes shut;
Nor in womb, I did have pain,
But you; so that I did gain;

Witnessed I on one morrow a cow,
Milking its calf with its head bow;
Remembered I the milking of you,
My life, if not you then who?

Because of you, I grew more,
Because of you I reached high shore;

Dear Diary

Neha Trivedi

Dear diary,

you're the sky to the stars that I paint in ink,

The one confidant who has seen blood, tears and the pitiless agony within. You've my merry chuckles, love drenched sighs, heartbreak tales and fake smiles, all tight-lippedly embraced in,

And I love how you cherish the ghastly demon that hides under my skin.

The dry petrichor fragrance that you wear, comes to my rescue when the

anxiety breaks in,

Dear diary,

you're not just crumbled blotted pages,

you're my soul-twin.

Dravid

K. Karthik

You Dravid,
Dravid, Dravid!!!
Wall, you Dravid,
Wall never falls.

You nice south Indian boy,
Never say to us bye;
Entered you to our team,
That so we Indians get esteem;
Played you always defense
That so opponent got annoyance.

Once got the Man of the Match,
Then got the Man of the Series,
Nearing one and only Man of India,
406 are what you did catch
In both ODIs and test series,
Is there any better Paiya

Than you? You the best keeper,
Never played you the sweeper.

Always your bat got fired,
That so opponent got tired;
Always your shot reached boundaries,
That so opponent captains got worries.

Always played you as opener,
That so India got Winner;
You Dravid is the match winner,
Never did you get out sooner.

Century number is thirty six,
Why you never hit more six?
Centuries in ODIs are twelve,
Always played you involve.

You, in future, be Indian coacher,
So we'll get best cricket preacher.

Rain

K. Karthik

It's hard, now-a day, to see you,
Almost you have gone elsewhere;
It's hard to the world to find you,
All these days, where are you?

Coming, once in a year or two,
Farmers in their fields, wanting you,
Children on the street, seeking you,
People in the world, waiting for you.

Once you come, we forget ourselves,
Dancing, singing, jumping along you;
I don't know where the hell you are,
Wherever you are, come here too;

Your good name is rain,
Come here and give gain...

Caste

K. Karthik

To admit me, my parents took me to school,
They, the educated illiterates, called us fool;
Because they asked our caste,
My parents replied with haste.

Asked us, "With that caste how?"
So we, before them, did bow;
Got into the class with fear,
To sit there, among my peer.

In class, I was not their favor,
All was nothing but my color;
Shared everything among their dears,
Left me alone, in eyes, with tears.

People do say I am educated,
But, I was, there, really punished;
They never taught us subject,
Only that ugly unseen object.

I like others, born with same red blood, Then why I, suffocating in caste flood?

Walk with Me

Abhijith Mohan

Walk with me,
Under the clouds curious.
For they know nothing,
about staying forever.
Walk with me,
Under shades of spring.
For they believe,
In rejoicing.
Walk with me,
To the shores of sand,
For the sea is adventure,
A forbidden fruit.
Walk with me,
To moon and back.
We'll let the stars be free,
From the burden of wishes.

You who gave me the first Crush

K. Karthik

This feeling, in the world, comes as usual,
To me also, once come with casual;
That is what others say, “Love”,
Love is something that is to give.

I too gave, my first half to her,
Cared she, my heart became her,
Her gorgeous heart became mine,
Life, with her went on fine.

Wherever I was, she was there,
I went with my girl everywhere;
My world, to me, she did become,
To my world, had nothing come

Only she; before me she stood,
So that, I did, what others never could;
Said she, will be with me
Forever; I will suffer without she.

But on one unfortunate bitter day,
She came and cuddled without gay,
Said, she is going and does cry,
And cry, to make my life dry.

Hell

K. Karthik

All the ways go to the prosperous land,
But I'm standing only in the 'waste land';
Traveling towards a particular place,
Without knowing the ultimate cause.

To stand in a desert is eerie,
Come, I like a deserted palm tree,
Almost like a rolling lengthy stone,
Walking to and fro lone.

I'm dying like a fish without
Water; trying to come out
of the hell-like dirty pond,
Where there is no respond.

Seen you, in life, any caricature?
If not, come to me and capture;
Because, no one in the world,
Does stand like me without a word.

The moon, in my place, is not a moon,
You'll understand it very soon;
Stars, here, are not stars,
But, for me, they are scars.

Some says, 'There is no hell',
But I say, he is only a fool;
Some says, 'Where there's a will,
There's a way,' no way, only hell.

Please come and pick me up,
If you do, you are really superb.

Myself with Me

Aayush Jaiswal

Sometimes in this world I feel like being alone

Just to get rid of all my agonies, my delusions and being of my own. Sometimes in this world I feel like to eradicate all fears

move to a place, quiet and clear where I need not to hide my tears. Sometimes in this world I feel like

I have died even when I'm in front of everyone's eyes But I know I have nothing inside.

Sometimes in this world I feel like to diminish But for my beloved ones, I am here to flourish. Still sometimes in this world I feel like to be Alone.

The Act

Abhijith Mohan

The curtains fell once again.

The performance was over.

But the claps and applause were so far away, they were not real to me. All I could see was the mirror,

All I could see were the cracks, all I felt was the pain in my bruised knuckles.

I watched myself in silence, as I took off the mask.

It was glorious,

The scars were shining,

It was beautiful.

But,

Only to me.

Peacock

K. Karthik

Once in our garden, I searched
For you; because ere I captured
By your beauty, immense beauty,
Which everyone wonders with piety.

Simple you are, in visual,
Compound you are, in complexion,
Complex you are, in pride,
Exquisite you are, beyond all words.

You, our great national bird,
Capturing the eyes of three-third,
The place where you stand,
Will have people of grand.

When you, with your feather dance,
We see without taking our glance;
From us whenever you flies,
We look with regret eyes.

Can't you fly very high,
Having in your heart no shy;
These things make our heart,
For you, to feel die-hard.

Not only Me but also You

K. Karthik

I won't say it's not my mistake,
It's you too who offer me to take;
Only you asked me to stay,
But now you say, you would slay.

Of course, I disturbed you so,
I don't know how to show
My love; I won't justify,
But you too don't crucify.

Many times I lean against your shoulder,
Because I nowhere get shelter;
Please don't mistake me dear,
If you don't, I can't bear.

I know you now forget,
To get you back is my target;
Ere informing my mistakes to others,
Do think I am yours.

Hereafter, for me, you don't cry,
No, no. I won't make you cry

Father's Day

Aayush Jaiswal

From holding my fingertip to holding my hands at fare. From teaching me how to cycle to warning me to drive slow

From taking me on your shoulder to taking my shoulder as your staff.

You have always armed me from the storm of world and armed you're your courage to fight.

Relishing a single day cannot justify all this because our each conversation turns out to be Father's Day.

I Believe Now

Abhijith Mohan

A cynic I was, undaunted by the eyes.
As a rebel I lived, jumping into fathoms forbidden.
Fear didn't touch me, for I was mine.
Then she came, with her star filled eyes.
Making me wonder about the constellations above.
I believe now.
I believe in magic.

To Love and To be Loved

K. Karthi

Many asks me to do something,
Except loving her, I know nothing;
With her, I remain her anytime,
To do something, I have no time.

She opens her eyes and smiles,
This takes me to far miles;
When she turns, I am turned over,
I want her to be with me forever.

My life is not my life,
Until she becomes my wife;
It's love at first sight,
I want her within my site.

I don't want her to speak,
When she does so, I become weak;
She says, "you are my half-friend,"
I want her to take to other end.

It is all her action,

That makes me no motion;

It's all her cute expression,

That gives me too much impression.

I do write now a poem,

It's she who shows who I am.